how2become

KS2 SCIENCE IS EASY

PHYSICS

THE
REVISION
SERIES

www.How2Become.com

As part of this product you have also received FREE access to online tests that will help you to pass Key Stage 2 SCIENCE *(Physics)*.

To gain access, simply go to:

www.PsychometricTestsOnline.co.uk

Get more products
for passing any test at:

www.How2Become.com

Orders: Please contact How2Become Ltd, Suite 14, 50 Churchill Square Business Centre, Kings Hill, Kent ME19 4YU.

You can order through Amazon.co.uk under ISBN 9781910602928, via the website www.How2Become.com or through Gardners.com.

ISBN: 9781910602928

First published in 2016 by How2Become Ltd.

Typeset for How2Become Ltd by Anton Pshinka.

Disclaimer

Every effort has been made to ensure that the information contained within this guide is accurate at the time of publication. How2Become Ltd is not responsible for anyone failing any part of any selection process as a result of the information contained within this guide. How2Become Ltd and their authors cannot accept any responsibility for any errors or omissions within this guide, however caused. No responsibility for loss or damage occasioned by any person acting, or refraining from action, as a result of the material in this publication can be accepted by How2Become Ltd.

The information within this guide does not represent the views of any third party service or organisation.

CONTENTS

THE
REVISION
SERIES

GUIDANCE
FOR PARENTS

Whilst the SATs are a daunting, disliked and often maligned concept, they remain an essential part of a child's education. Children should be provided with the best tools and guidance to enhance their intellectual ability and improve their performance.

The purpose of this section is to guide you through the KS2 Science (Physics) exam. It will allow you to familiarise yourself with all of the important information, advice and tips that your child will need in order to achieve exam success.

The NEW SATs

From the summer of 2016, the SATs will have undergone considerable changes, as dictated by the new national curriculum.

The purpose of the new and revised SATs is to ensure these tests remain rigorous, and therefore prove to be of a much higher standard compared to previous years.

With the new national curriculum comes a new marking scheme. Whilst we cannot provide details of exactly what this marking scheme consists of, we know that your child's tests will be marked externally. The scores of these tests will be used to monitor the progress of each school's performance, which is done via Ofsted reports and League tables.

Ultimately, your child's scores in their SATs will be used in conjunction with classroom assessments, to provide a general overview of their attainment and progression during that academic year.

For more information on the new national curriculum, please visit the Department for Education section of the Government's website.

When Do the New SATs Come into Place?

The new national curriculum for Key Stage 2 SATs will have been assessed for the first time in May 2016.

What do the New SATs Cover?

The national curriculum for Key Stage 2 SATs will consist of the following:

- English Reading (Comprehension);
- English Grammar (Grammar, Punctuation and Spelling);
- Maths (Arithmetic and Reasoning);
- Science (Biology, Chemistry, Physics)*.

*(*Please note that not all children completing the SATs will sit a Science SAT. A selection of schools will be required to take part in a science sampling every other year.)*

For more revision guides including KS2 Biology and Chemistry, as well as KS2 Science Practice Papers, please visit www.How2Become.com.

Top Tips For Parents

In order for your child to score highly in their SATs, you need to ensure that they have everything they need to achieve high marks!

It is important that you and your child are fully aware of what the SATs consist of. The more familiar you are with what to expect, the better their chances will be when they sit down to take the tests.

Below is a list of GOLDEN NUGGETS that will help you AND your child to prepare for the Key Stage 2 SATs.

- ## Golden Nugget 1 – Revision timetables

When it comes to exams, preparation is key. That is why you need to sit down with your child and come up with an efficient and well-structured revision timetable.

It is important that you work with your child to assess their academic strengths and weaknesses, in order to carry out these revision sessions successfully.

TIP – *Focus on their weaker areas first!*

TIP – *Create a weekly revision timetable to work through different subject areas.*

TIP – *Spend time revising with your child. Your child will benefit from your help and this is a great way for you to monitor their progress.*

- ## Golden Nugget 2 – Understanding the best way your child learns

There are many different ways to revise when it comes to exams, and it all comes down to picking a way that your child will find most useful.

Below is a list of the common learning styles that you may want to try with your child:

- **Visual** – the use of pictures and images to remember information.

- **Aural** – the use of sound and music to remember information.

- **Verbal** – the use of words, in both speech and writing, to understand information.

- **Social** – working together in groups.

- **Solitary** – working and studying alone.

Popular revision techniques include: *mind mapping, flash cards, making notes, drawing flow charts* and *diagrams.* You could instruct your child on how to turn diagrams and pictures into words, and words into diagrams. Try as many different methods as possible to see which is the most successful for your child's learning.

TIP – Work out what kind of learner your child is. What method will they benefit from the most?

TIP – Try a couple of different learning aids and see if you notice a change in your child's ability to understand what is being taught.

• Golden Nugget 3 – Break times

Allow your child plenty of breaks when revising.

It's really important not to overwork your child, particularly for tests such as the SATs which are not marked on a pass or fail basis.

TIP – Practising for 10 to 15 minutes per day will improve your child's understanding of the topic being revised.

• Golden Nugget 4 – Practice, practice and more practice!

Purchase past practice papers. Although the curriculum will have changed for 2016, practice papers are still a fantastic way for you to gain an idea of how your child is likely to be tested.

- ## Golden Nugget 5 – Variety is key!

Make sure that your child reads a VARIETY of different physics modules. This will be required if they wish to score high marks overall on their Science exam.

> *TIP – Spend some time with your child and write a list of all the key areas and topics that need to be covered. This way, your child will be able to tailor their revision to each module and achieve a broad understanding of the curriculum.*

- ## Golden Nugget 6 – Encourage your child to discuss their work

When your child is undergoing practice questions, ask your child to talk about what they have just learned. Did they understand it? Did they know what all the words meant?

> *TIP – Sit down with your child and ask them questions about what they have just learnt. Have they understood everything? Is there anything they're unsure of?*

- ## Golden Nugget 7 – Stay positive!

The most important piece of preparation advice we can give you is to make sure that your child is positive and relaxed about these tests.

Don't let the SATs worry you, and certainly don't let them worry your child.

> *TIP – Make sure the home environment is as comfortable and relaxed as possible for your child.*

- ## Golden Nugget 8 – Answer the easier questions first

A good tip to teach your child is to answer all the questions they find easiest first. That way, they can swiftly work through the questions before attempting the questions they struggle with.

TIP – Get your child to undergo a practice paper. Tell them to fill in the answers that they find the easiest first. That way, you can spend time helping your child with the questions they find more difficult.

Spend some time working through the questions they find difficult and make sure that they know how to work out the answer.

- ## Golden Nugget 9 – Take a look at our other Science revision guides

How2Become have also created other Science revision guides to help you prepare for other sciences including Chemistry and Biology. Be sure to check out these other revision guides for more practice questions and information.

THE
REVISION
SERIES

LIGHT

LIGHT

In this first chapter, we'll focus on the topic of light! Light is the only thing that makes sight possible, and only comes from a few sources.

With the help of our superhero Preston, we will learn what light is, how it moves, and how it makes you see!

These are the topic headings for this chapter:

1. **Light and dark**

2. **Shadows**

3. **How we see**

It's lit!

LIGHT

1. Light and dark

Light allows us to see things – your eyes use the light that bounces off what you are looking at to make sight possible. Dark is the absence of light.

Most light comes from one main source – THE SUN. Sunlight takes about 8 minutes to reach Earth. During night-time, whichever part of Earth you are on has rotated away from the Sun. So, it cannot receive direct sunlight, making it dark outside.

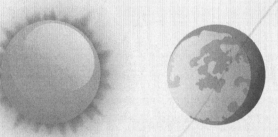

While the Sun is a source of light, the moon is not. Moonlight exists, but it is actually just reflected light originating from the Sun.

Remember, looking directly at the Sun will severely damage your eyes, even if you're wearing sunglasses. Don't do it! The Sun is too powerful!

LIGHT

Of course, there are other sources of light in everyday life, such as lightbulbs, candles, phone screens and televisions. Inventions such as these have made seeing things at night-time possible.

How light behaves

Light only travels in straight lines, and will reflect off of any material – although some materials reflect more light than others. Light will reflect off the surface at the same angle at which it hit the surface. So, it is possible to use shiny things to aim beams of light, like with a ruler in a classroom!

Different things will happen to light depending on the properties of the material it encounters:

* Smooth, shiny, and light-coloured surfaces...
   o Will reflect a lot of light.
   o This makes them useful for things like mirrors, which let us see ourselves (our reflections!), behind us or around corners.
   o Reflective surfaces also help us be seen in the dark.

Equal Angles of Reflection

LIGHT

- Rough, dull, and dark-coloured surfaces...

  o Will reflect very little light – will absorb light, stopping it from travelling.

  o This makes them useful for blinds and curtains; anything where light needs to be blocked out.

2. Shadows

Shadows form when something opaque or translucent blocks direct light, creating shade.

Transparent objects will not cause a shadow to form.

Shadows are the same shape as the objects they form from.

> Transparent materials: Allow light to pass through them – like a window made of clear glass.
>
> Translucent materials: Allow some light to pass through them – like a green glass bottle.
>
> Opaque materials: Allow no light to pass through them – like the wood of a tree's trunk.

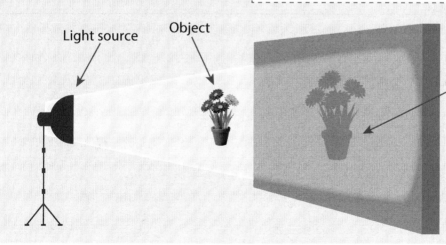

Light source   Object   Shadow

LIGHT

It is possible to change the size of a shadow.

For example, the closer an object is to the light source, the larger the shadow will be. So, the further away an object is to a light source, the smaller the shadow will be.

Sun shadows

Of course, as the major source of light in our lives, the Sun casts shadows. See below for the shadows cast by the Sun as it rises and sets. For more detail on sunrises and sunsets, see page 80.

1. In the morning, the Sun rises in the East. So, initially, people and objects cast a long shadow on Earth, because of the low position of the Sun.

2. Shadows on Earth grow gradually shorter as the Sun reaches its highest point (at 12pm midday). At midday, shadows become as short as they'll get at any other time.

3. After midday, the Sun begins to set, finally doing so in the West. Shadows become longer and longer as the day draws to a close. They now face the other direction, as the Sun is now on the opposite side of the sky.

3. How we see

Recap:

- We need light to see;
- Light travels in straight lines;
- Everything reflects light, but some things do so more than others.

The above points are all very important things to know before we learn how humans are able to see.

The way we see can be broken down into three steps:

Step 1: Light travels from a light source (e.g. the Sun or a lightbulb) towards whatever you're looking at. Let's say that you're looking at a book.

Step 2: The light (always travelling in a straight line) hits the book, which reflects it towards your eyes.

Step 3: The light enters your eyes, which converts the light into impulses which are sent to the brain – which tells you what you see!

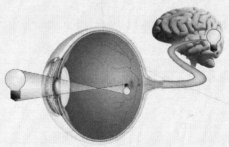

Question 1

Answer the following questions by circling one of the three options given: **always**, **sometimes**, or **never**.

a) Earth receives light from the Sun.

ALWAYS	SOMETIMES	NEVER

b) The moon produces light.

ALWAYS	SOMETIMES	NEVER

c) The Sun shines on London.

ALWAYS	SOMETIMES	NEVER

d) You should look directly at the Sun.

ALWAYS	SOMETIMES	NEVER

e) Light travels in straight lines.

ALWAYS	SOMETIMES	NEVER

f) You can see without light.

ALWAYS	SOMETIMES	NEVER

Question 2

Scarlett is creating an experiment to demonstrate that light reflects from surfaces at the same angle at which it enters surfaces. The equipment for this experiment includes a torch, a protractor, and an upright mirror.

The first thing Scarlett does is set up the mirror so it stands perpendicular to the protractor resting on a table:

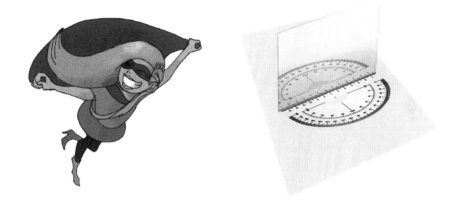

The next step Scarlett will take is to turn the lights off.

Scarlett then shines the torch's thin beam at the centre (origin) of the protractor from the 50° (degree) line.

The torch beam hits the mirror just above the centre of the protractor, and is reflected.

At what angle will the beam be reflected to on the other side of the protractor?

Give your answer in degrees, using this symbol: °.

How do you know this?

_____

_____

_____

Question 3

In the box is a selection of different materials, and some properties of the materials. Below the box is a list of possible uses of these materials.

Put **one** material in all the boxes next to each possible use.

> **Smooth, shiny glass**
>
> **Bright-coloured, shiny vinyl**
>
> **Clear glass**
>
> **Opaque, rough cloth**

a) A row of windows for a school.

b) A mirror in a hairdresser's salon.

c) A black backdrop for a photographer's studio.

d) A hi-visibility jacket for a builder on a construction site.

Question 4

Anil has three materials; **material A**, **material B** and **material C**. He wants to prove which one is transparent, which one is translucent, and which one is opaque. To make it a fair test, he uses the same torch and shines it from the same distance at all three materials. He then examines what kind of shadows they cast. This is what he recorded:

Shadows cast

Material A: Casts no shadow

Material B: Casts a sharp, completely black shadow

Material C: Casts a blurry, greyish shadow

Help Anil decide which material is which by writing **transparent**, **translucent** or **opaque** in each of the three boxes below.

Material A:

Material B:

Material C:

Question 5

Freddie is investigating how objects' shadows change, depending on the position of the light source acting on the object. He plans to aim a lamp at a Rubik's cube from three different distances, and observe how the shadows cast on the wall change from each position.

Position 1 of the lamp will be 3 metres from the Rubik's cube. Position 2 will be 2 metres from the Rubik's cube. Position 3 will be 1 metre from the Rubik's cube.

a) To make it a fair test, Freddie will keep the Rubik's cube the same distance from the wall each time the lamp is moved. Name two other ways he can ensure that he carries out a fair test.

_____

_____

b) How do you expect the size of the shadow to change from position to position? What could the conclusion of this test be?

_____

_____

c) How would you suggest Freddie measures the sizes of the shadows cast?

_____

_____

Question 6

Match the descriptions of three times of day to the boxes reading 'Sunrise', 'Sunset' and 'Midday' by drawing lines between them.

| The Sun is at its highest point, shadows cast are very short. |

SUNRISE

| The Sun is very low and in the East, causing long shadows pointing to the West. |

SUNSET

| The Sun is very low and in the West, causing long shadows pointing to the East. |

MIDDAY

Question 7

Lalita is looking at a basketball. Using a ruler and a protractor, draw two lines on the picture, with arrows to show direction, showing the movement of light which makes this possible.

| Lalita | Object | Light source |

ANSWERS TO LIGHT

Question 1

a) Always

b) Never

c) Sometimes

d) Never

e) Always

f) Never

Question 2

50°

Light is always reflected away at the same angle at which it hits a surface. Therefore, it is possible to know that the light would be reflected away at 50° in Scarlett's experiment, because we were told that the beam would be introduced to the mirror at angle of 50°.

Question 3

a) Clear glass

b) Smooth, shiny glass

c) Opaque, rough cloth

d) Bright-coloured, shiny vinyl

Question 4

Material A: Transparent

Material B: Opaque

Material C: Translucent

Question 5

a) To ensure that he carries out a fair test, Freddie should use the same lamp with the same bulb throughout the experiment. He must also use the same Rubik's cube each time.

b) Position 1 of the lamp, when the lamp is furthest from the cube, will produce the smallest shadow on the wall. Position 2 will produce a bigger shadow. Position three will produce the biggest shadow on the wall. So, the closer the lamp gets to the wall, the shadow cast by the cube will increase.

c) Freddie should measure the size of the shadows cast with a ruler, finding the width and length of the shadows cast.

Question 6

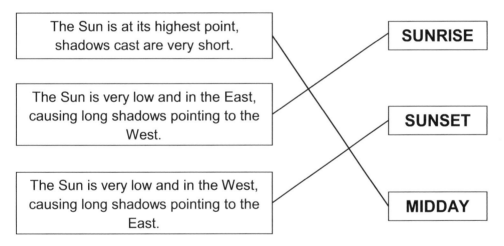

Question 7

THE
REVISION
SERIES

SOUND

SOUND

In this chapter, we will focus on light's slightly less important and much slower cousin, sound. With the help of our superhero Anil, we will learn what sound is and how it moves.

<u>Here are the main three topics of this chapter:</u>

1. **What is sound?**

2. **Sound travel**

3. **Sound features**

Sounds like a plan!

SOUND

1. What is sound?

A sound is produced when something vibrates. For example, when a guitar string is plucked, its movement affects the air and sends vibrations towards your ears. This vibration travels into your ear, which is able to process the sound and tell your brain what noise was made. The speed of sound is many times slower than the speed of light.

Human speech

A human is able to speak and make noise with his/her larynx (voice box), located in the throat. The larynx produces vibrations, and therefore sounds, when air passes through it. These vibrations are directed to come out of the mouth, so humans can control them to produce complicated speech.

SOUND

2. Sound travel

Sound can also travel through solids and liquids, as they are able to carry vibrations as well. Sound actually travels faster through solids and liquids than it does through air and other gases.

Of course, some materials are better carriers of sound than others, and some things are designed to stop sound travelling.

Sound and vacuums

Sound needs something to travel through in order to reach your ears, because a vibration cannot travel through nothing – it needs a **medium** to carry it. This means that sound cannot travel through a vacuum. For example, sound cannot travel through outer space.

The bell is ringing, but it is held in a vacuum so it cannot be heard.

SOUND

3. Sound features

Pitch

A sound's pitch refers to how high or low a sound is. That is to say, the more high-pitched a sound is, the squeakier it is. So, the more low-pitched a sound is, the deeper it is.

On a guitar for example, shorter strings will produce higher pitched sounds than longer strings. Different pitches cause different musical notes.

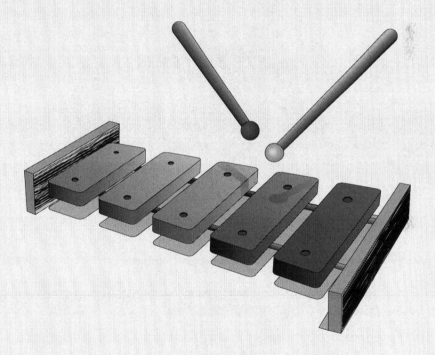

Similarly, on a glockenspiel, the longer keys produce deeper notes than the shorter keys. This is because a smaller key produces faster vibrations.

SOUND

Loudness

The loudness of a sound refers to its volume and intensity. The opposite of 'loud' in this case is not 'quiet' as you might expect, but 'soft'.

In the case of the instruments mentioned on the previous page, the amount of force you apply to a string or key will affect the loudness of sound produced.

The loudness of a sound is measured in decibels (dB).

Question 1

Answer the multiple choice questions by circling either **a)**, **b)** or **c)**.

1. What are sounds?

    a. Vibrations

    b. Radiation waves

    c. Currents

2. How do humans' voice boxes produce sound?

    a. Electrical vibrations

    b. Muscles working on their own

    c. Air rushes through them

3. Sound travels fastest through…

    a. Solids

    b. Gases

    c. Liquids

4. Sound can travel through vacuums…

    a. Always

    b. Never

    c. Sometimes

Question 2

Anil knows that hitting the longer keys on a xylophone will produce a deeper sound than hitting the shorter keys. He wants to find out how the pitch of the sound made by hitting his drum can be changed.

The first thing he does is tighten the skin of his drum. This will cause the drum skin to vibrate more quickly when hit. He hits the drum.

Next, he loosens the skin of his drum even more so than how it was when he started. This will cause the drum skin to vibrate more slowly when hit. He hits the drum.

Which drum beat produces the lower sound, drumbeat 1 or drumbeat 2?

Put a tick in **one** box.

Drumbeat 1   Drumbeat 2

Explain your choice.

_____

_____

_____

_____

Question 3

Freddie is playing his trumpet and measuring the amount of decibels he produces with different strength blasts. He records his findings in the following table:

Trumpet blast	Decibels produced
1	65
2	81
3	92

Answer the following questions about Freddie's test:

a) From his results, how do you think Freddie changed his trumpet blasts from 1-3?

_____

_____

b) How does increasing the strength of his trumpet blasts affect the number of decibels the trumpet sound produced?

_____

_____

c) How does the amount of decibels produced by a sound relate to how loud a sound is?

_____

_____

ANSWERS TO SOUND

Question 1

1. a. Vibrations

2. c. Air rushes through them

3. a. Solids

4. b. Never

Question 2

Drumbeat 2.

Drumbeat 2 will produce a lower sound because a looser drum skin will vibrate slower than a tight drum skin. This means that the sound is formed of slower vibrations, meaning it is low-pitched.

Question 3

a) Freddie increased the strength of his trumpet blasts from 1-3. 1 was the softest blast and 3 was the hardest blast.

b) The harder Freddie blew into the trumpet, the more decibels its sound produced.

c) The more decibels a sound produces, the louder the sound will be.

HOW ARE YOU GETTING ON?

THE
REVISION
SERIES

ELECTRICITY

ELECTRICITY

This section will cover all things electrical; the current affairs if you will. With the help of superhero Freddie, we will look at some everyday uses of electricity, and start to look at how circuits work!

We will do so in three main sections:

1. **Electricity around the house**

2. **Conductors and insulators**

3. **Circuits**

ELECTRICITY

1. Electricity around the house

We use electricity to provide power to devices and appliances that need it to work. We use electricity every day for many different things, at home and at school. It is easy to take it for granted, but it is worth remembering that human-controlled electricity has not always existed; its invention changed our lives forever.

We access electricity through the mains – where you plug devices and appliances in. So, everything from your toaster to your phone charger needs electricity power to work.

Electricity can harm us, because human bodies are able to conduct electricity! So, if we inadvertently complete a circuit by exposing ourselves to the electrical energy, we can receive a nasty shock.

Toasters need electrical power to get hot and toast bread, and phone chargers are able to supply electrical energy to your phone to give it power.

For electricity to flow, it needs a complete circuit. Any gaps or breaks in the circuit will result in a loss of power.

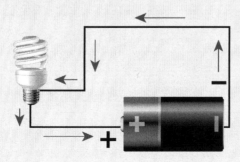

We will look at circuits in more detail later!

ELECTRICITY

2. Conductors and insulators

Some materials are better at conducting electricity than others, and some materials cannot conduct electricity at all.

For example, many metals are good conductors of electricity – they allow electricity to pass through them very quickly, and can complete electrical currents, making them useful to humans in a variety of situations where electricity is required. Copper wires are used to provide power to electrical appliances.

The opposite of a conductor is called an insulator – something that prevents electricity from flowing through it. These are also very useful to humans, for very different reasons.

For example, rubber is used to coat metal wires to stop electricity being transferred to our bodies and harming us when we are plugging things in! Materials like wood and plastic are also electrical insulators.

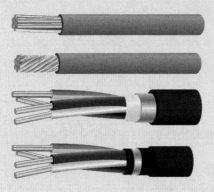

3. Circuits

As mentioned before, electricity cannot supply things with power without a complete circuit (one with no gaps). And, to turn a lightbulb on for example, a circuit needs to have a source of power, like a battery.

This picture shows a complete circuit with a cell (single battery), and lit bulb:

A broken circuit, even with a power source, will not make a lightbulb turn on:

REMEMBER!

Always take care when working with electrical circuits; make sure you have an adult supervising your activity!

ELECTRICITY

<u>Circuit symbols</u>

In a scientific diagram, different components of a circuit are represented with different symbols. These allow us to draw circuits even if we aren't very artistic!

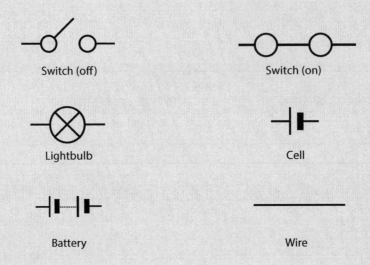

Switch (off)   Switch (on)

Lightbulb   Cell

Battery   Wire

Here is an example of a circuit containing a closed switch, a lit light bulb, and a cell, drawn using scientific symbols.

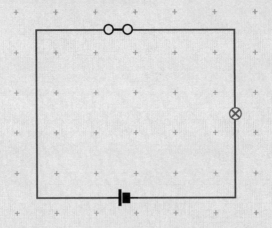

Considering what you've just learned, do you think the bulb would light up if the switch was open?

Different circuits

It is important to know that there are many things you can change in a circuit that will affect the amount of power it supplies to its components.

In other words, in a simple circuit with a lightbulb, there are things you can add, take away, or change that will affect how brightly the bulb will shine.

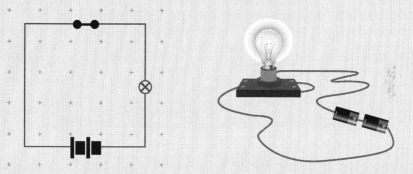

For example, adding more cells will make the bulb shine brighter. Adding too many cells will cause the bulb to stop working or even blow; it is possible to provide components with too much electricity!

Adding more bulbs will cause the light given off to be dimmer. This is because the same amount of electrical energy in the circuit must now power twice the amount of components.

ELECTRICITY

Similarly, the length of wire in a circuit will affect the amount of power it is able to supply to components like bulbs, motors or buzzers. If long wires are used to construct a circuit, less energy will be supplied to the components. This is because the electricity has to spend energy travelling the longer distance to the things that need supplying.

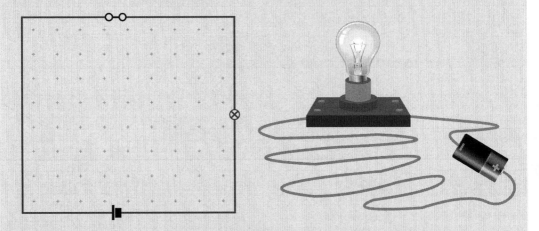

Look at the circuit below. Will it work? Why/why not?

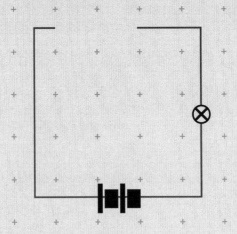

Question 1

In the boxes below are a list of statements about electricity and how we use it in our everyday lives. But, some of them are incorrect. Put a tick (✔) in the boxes next to the true statements, and a cross (✘) in the boxes next to the wrong statements.

Humans have always used electricity to help them around the house or at school.	
Devices like computers need electrical power to work.	
Electrical circuits need to be complete in order to supply power to things.	
Every material is able to conduct electricity efficiently.	
In an electrical circuit, some energy is always lost through sound and heat energy.	
Electricity has the potential to harm us.	

Question 2

For people who work with electricity, it is of vital importance that they protect themselves from shocks.   Using words like 'conductor' and 'insulator', describe how they might do this.

_____

_____

_____

_____

_____

_____

_____

Question 3

Anil is creating some simple circuits using cells, wires, switches, lightbulbs and buzzers. Answer the following multiple choice questions, by circling **a)**, **b)** or **c)** about what happens when he changes his circuit:

1. Anil constructs a circuit using wires, a cell, a lightbulb and a switch. He leaves the switch open.

    The bulb will be:

    a) Illuminated brightly

    b) Lit dimly

    c) Off

2. Next, he closes the switch.

    The bulb is now:

    a) On

    b) Off

    c) Broken

3. He then adds another cell, so the circuit contains a battery.

The light produced by the bulb now shines:

a) Brighter

b) Dimmer

c) At the same strength

4. The next thing he does is add more wires to his circuit, making it run longer.

a) This will not affect the brightness of the bulb

b) This will make the bulb shine brighter

c) This will make the bulb shine dimmer

5. Anil then replaces the long wires with short ones, and adds three more cells. The lightbulb is very small.

a) The bulb shines dimmer

b) The bulb receives too much power, and does not light up

c) The switch opens

6. Finally, he replaces the lightbulb with a buzzer, takes out three cells and completes the circuit.

a) When switched on, the buzzer will produce sound

b) The buzzer will not make any sound

c) The lightbulb will explode

ANSWERS TO ELECTRICITY

Question 1

Humans have always used electricity to help them around the house or at school.	
Devices like computers need electrical power to work.	
Electrical circuits need to be complete in order to supply power to things.	
Every material is able to conduct electricity efficiently.	
In an electrical circuit, some energy is always lost through sound and heat energy.	
Electricity has the potential to harm us.	

Question 2

Human bodies are good conductors of electricity, so those who are working near powerful circuits need to take steps to make sure they do not expose themselves to the electrical energy. They can do this by using tools and wearing clothes that are electrical insulators, which will form a barrier between the electrical power and their bodies.

Question 3

1. c)

2. a)

3. a)

4. b)

5. a)

HOW ARE YOU GETTING ON? 👍 👎 👎

THE
REVISION
SERIES

FORCES

FORCES

In this chapter, we will talk about the natural forces at work in our world and indeed our universe. Scarlett, another of our superheroes, will be on hand to guide us through!

She will do so in three main sections:

1. **Gravity**

2. **Forces of resistance**

3. **Levers, pulleys, and gears**

Irresistible!

FORCES

Forces are constantly happening all around us. A force can be described as a push or pull that causes motion. But, even when objects are still, forces are still acting upon them; it is when forces are unbalanced that objects will move.

1. Gravity

Gravity is a constant force in our universe. It holds planets in their round shapes, and keeps them in orbit around the Sun. Gravity is the force that keeps you on the ground here on Earth, and contains our atmosphere so we can breathe.

Gravity acts towards the centre of all stars and planets.

In everyday life, gravity is the force that makes objects fall to the ground if they are unsupported.

Gravity is also what gives you weight, which means the amount of force that gravity is exerting on you. This is why you would weigh less on the moon, where the force of gravity acts more weakly! Weight is measured in newtons using a force meter.

Weight is different to mass, which is a measure of how many particles an object is made out of, so be careful! Mass can be measured in kilograms.

FORCES

2. Forces of resistance

Friction

Friction is the force that slows and stops the movement of an object sliding across another object. For example, friction is the reason it is difficult to push your sofa across your carpet. This would also produce heat. Without friction, objects pushed across a floor would slide forever.

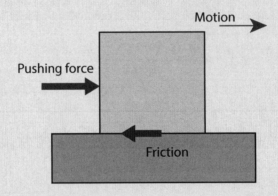

Of course, some surfaces cause more friction than others; rougher materials will produce more friction than smoother materials when something rubs against them.

In some situations, it is useful to maximise the amounts of friction produced. For example, friction between the brakes of your bike and the tyres allow you to control when you stop.

Equally, it is sometimes useful to minimise the amounts of friction produced. Imagine trying to ice skate without the smooth edges of the blades on your shoes!

FORCES

Air resistance

Air resistance is a type of friction that acts on things that are flying or falling through the air. Backwards force is generated when an object is moving and making contact with the atoms in the air. Air resistance means that planes need to use extra fuel to generate the power needed to move quickly through the air.

Thrust

Air resistance

This friction can be minimised by streamlining – adapting an object's shape to allow air to pass over it more easily.

Water resistance

Similarly, water resistance is the type of friction generated when objects are moving through water. Atoms in water are closer together than they are in gases, so water resistance will produce a greater backwards force on an object than the same object would face while moving through air.

Drag

Thrust

FORCES

3. Levers, pulleys, and gears

Levers, pulleys, and gears are all technically machines – they allow us to exert big forces with little effort. This is because they are designed to multiply the force that is put into them, and put a bigger force out.

Levers

Levers are able to reduce the amount of force required to lift or move objects. This is done by increasing the distance through which the force acts, which multiplies it. Look at the diagram below. Imagine the platform was longer, and the arrow (representing force) was further away from the triangle (the fulcrum). This would make it easier to lift the weight.

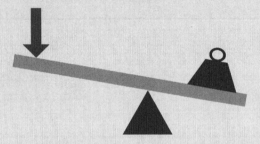

Pulleys

Pulleys make it easier to lift things by sharing the load between the person pulling and whatever the pulley is attached to – this could be a ceiling or any support structure. A simple pulley (shown below) will half the amount of force needed to lift the load; adding more pulleys to work together will diminish the effort required even more.

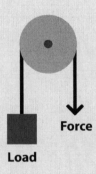

Force

Load

Gears

Gears are made up of at least two cogs that mesh together with their specially designed teeth. This means that it is possible to move multiple cogs while only supplying power to one.

Cogs are also able to multiply force between them. Imagine you have a large cog with 40 teeth, and a small cog with only 10 teeth. You mesh them together, then supply power to the large cog, making it turn. This also makes the small cog turn, but it does so 4 times as quickly as the large cog, because it has a quarter of the teeth and is a quarter of the size. The faster turning generates more force than what you have supplied to the large cog. You have made a gear!

Question 1

a) Name the force that causes objects to fall towards the ground.

_____

b) How is weight measured?

_____

c) Name three things that gravity does in our universe, solar system, and on Earth.

_____

_____

d) How is weight different to mass?

_____

_____

Question 2

Preston is examining how different materials produce different amounts of friction. He has a toy car, and three different strips of material of the same length. He plans to make the car roll across each type of material and measure how far each of them travels. The first material is a smooth pane of glass, the second is a plank of wood, and the third is a strip of carpet. The shorter the distance the car travels on a material, the more friction has been generated.

a) How can Preston ensure that he carries out a fair test?

_____

_____

b) Name three pieces of apparatus that Preston will need for this test.

_____

_____

c) Write out some step-by-step instructions that Preston could follow to carry out this experiment.

_____

_____

_____

_____

_____

_____

_____

_____

d) What do you expect the result of Preston's experiment to be?

_____

_____

_____

_____

Question 3

Answer the following questions by circling either **TRUE** or **FALSE**.

a) Levers, pulleys, and gears are able to multiply force they receive.

TRUE   **FALSE**

b) These machines are able to create force.

TRUE   **FALSE**

c) The closer the applied force is to the fulcrum of a lever, the bigger the resulting force will be.

TRUE   **FALSE**

d) A cog with 20 teeth will make a cog with 10 teeth turn twice as fast as it is turning.

TRUE   **FALSE**

ANSWERS TO FORCES

Question 1

a) Gravity

b) In newtons/With a forcemeter

c) Gravity holds planets and stars in their round shapes, keeps the Earth in orbit around the Sun, and makes things fall to the ground on Earth.

d) Weight is a measure of the amount of force gravity is exerting on something, while mass is a measure of the amount of particles of something, that does not change even when exposed to differing amounts of gravity.

Question 2

a) To ensure that he carries out a fair test, Preston should use the same car throughout, do multiple tests on each material, make sure the materials are the same size and make the cars move at the same speed by using the same ramp for each test.

b) Preston will need a toy car, a ruler to measure how far the car rolls, a ramp, and the three materials.

c) A possible list of instructions for this test could be:

- Set up the first material to be tested so it lies at the foot of the ramp.
- Place the car at the very top of the ramp or at a clearly marked line.
- Let the car roll down the ramp and across the material.
- From the foot of the ramp, measure how far the car rolled in centimetres.
- Record this result in a table.
- Repeat the last four steps another couple of times, and write down all the results.
- Repeat from step 1 with the other two materials.
- Write down a conclusion, describing your results and explaining how you made the test fair.

d) You should expect the car to travel the furthest on the glass surface, i.e. the glass produces the least amount of friction out of the three materials. You would also expect the carpet to produce the most amount of friction.

Question 3

a) TRUE

b) FALSE

c) FALSE

d) TRUE

MAGNETS

MAGNETS

In this chapter we will investigate the mysterious world of magnetism, including how magnets affect different materials. To help us get through this is superhero Lalita, who is here to share her wisdom!

We will look at magnets in three main sections:

1. **Magnetic force**

2. **Magnets and materials**

3. **Magnets in everyday life**

An attractive chapter...

MAGNETS

1. Magnetic force

Magnets produce magnetic fields. Although this is a natural phenomenon, humans are able to manufacture magnets for use in everyday life. Magnetic fields have a north and a south pole, so magnets do too. The Earth also produces a magnetic field – this is why we call its most northerly point the North Pole, and its most southerly point the South Pole!

North pole  South pole

The north pole of one magnet will attract to the south pole of another. In other words, opposite poles will attract, and matching poles will repel each other.

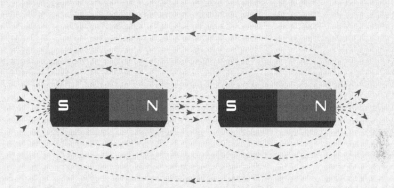

The south and north poles are attracted to each other
(will move towards each other).

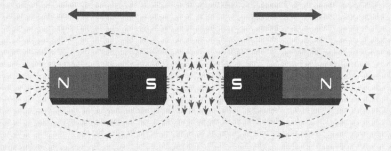

The south poles of the two magnets repel from each other (will move away from each other). This would also happen with the two north poles.

MAGNETS

2. Magnets and materials

As well as attracting each other, magnets are also able to attract certain types of materials, (**magnetic materials**) which are always metal. Magnets can make these materials move, which can be very helpful in many different industries.

A simple example of this would be if you made a paperclip move across a table using a small magnet. Metals containing iron (like steel) will be attracted by a magnetic pull.

However, a large number of metals are not magnetic. Precious metals like gold and silver will not be affected by a magnetic field, as well as other useful metals like aluminium and copper.

In sorting plants, magnets can be used to separate magnetic materials from non-magnetic materials.

MAGNETS

3. Magnets in everyday life

Magnets make up a vital part of a huge number of objects we use on a daily basis. For example, magnets are a key component of many electrical and electronic products, like computers, smartphones, and televisions. Bank cards also use a magnetic strip to transfer information to cash machines.

In transport, magnets are found in the engines of electric cars and are used in many electric functions of any car, such as automatic windows. Some trains even use extremely powerful magnets to float above the tracks! This allows them to reach extremely high speeds due to the massively reduced friction.

LAPTOP   **FLOATING BULLET TRAIN**

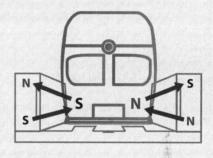

Simple magnets are used inside fridge doors to help keep them closed and preserve the temperature of the food. So, it's possible to say there are two types of fridge magnet!

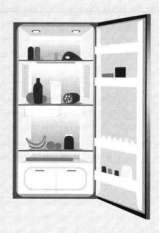

Question 1

a) What happens when the opposite poles of two magnets are near each other?

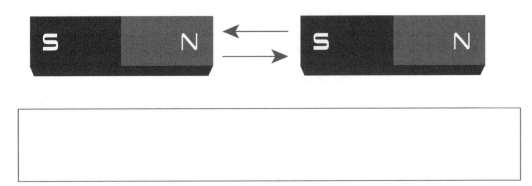

[blank answer box]

b) What happens when the same poles of two magnets are near each other?

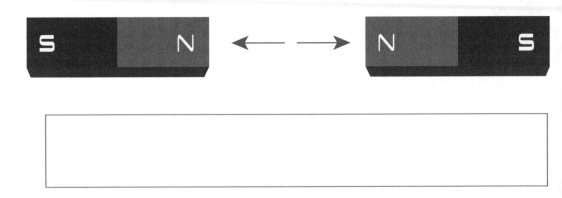

[blank answer box]

Question 2

Lalita has a box full of metal shavings after a recent metalwork project, in which she used two types of metal: steel and aluminium. She wants to sort them into two piles so she can properly dispose of them.

How could she do this?

_____

_____

_____

_____

_____

_____

Question 3

Use the box below to draw something magnetic that you use on a regular basis, either at school or at home. Also, write down why it is useful to you!

ANSWERS TO MAGNETS

Question 1

a) Attract

b) Repel

Question 2

Lalita could sort the two metals by taking advantage of the fact that steel is magnetic and aluminium is not. Placing a magnet inside the box will cause the steel shavings to be attracted to the magnet and stick to it. This will remove the steel shavings from the box while keeping the aluminium shavings inside.

Question 3

Your drawing could have depicted anything magnetic! Please ask a parent or guardian to check your answer.

HOW ARE YOU GETTING ON?

THE
REVISION
SERIES

EARTH

AND SPACE

EARTH AND SPACE

Our final chapter will attempt to tackle the greatest challenge of them all: outer space. We will look at how our planet moves around the Sun, the position of the Moon, and examine our solar system as a whole.

On hand with his evil genius is the villainous Blaze!

<u>This chapter will contain three main sections:</u>

1. **The solar system**

2. **The Earth and Moon**

3. **Human understanding of space**

EARTH AND SPACE

1. The solar system

The solar system refers to the collection of planets that Earth belongs to, as well as the star which they orbit – the Sun. Officially, there are 8 planets, which are all different sizes and located different distances away from the Sun – which is our closest star.

The planets are held in orbit by the gravitational pull of the Sun. As mentioned earlier in the book, the planets themselves (even the gas giants Jupiter, Saturn, Uranus and Neptune) are held in their near-spherical shapes by gravity.

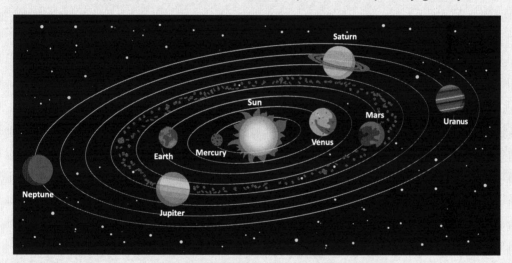

The order of the planets from the Sun is as follows:

(Use the **mnemonic** on the right-hand side to remember it!)

• Mercury – closest to the Sun.	➡ **My**
• Venus	➡ **Very**
• Earth	➡ **Easy**
• Mars	➡ **Method**
• Jupiter	➡ **Just**
• Saturn	➡ **Speeds**
• Uranus	➡ **Up**
• Neptune – furthest from the Sun.	➡ **Naming the planets!**

EARTH AND SPACE

2. The Earth and Moon

The Earth's orbit of the Sun

The Earth (where we live!) takes just over 365 days to complete a full orbit around the Sun. This is what we call a year.

During the course of this orbit, the Earth is constantly spinning on its axis. This gives us day and night – when the part of Earth (e.g. England) you are on is facing the Sun, you will be in daytime. So, when the part of Earth you are on has spun around to face away from the Sun, you will be in night-time.

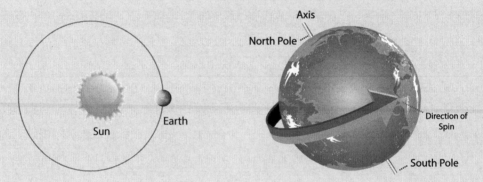

The seasons

During its journey around the Sun, the Earth stays tilted at the same angle the whole way round. This means that for half the year, the northern hemisphere of the Earth (where Europe is) is tilted towards the Sun, while the southern hemisphere is tilted away from the Sun. Therefore, during the other half of the year, when the Earth is on the opposite side of the Sun, the Southern hemisphere is tilted towards the Sun and the northern hemisphere is tilted away.

This phenomenon is what gives rise to our seasons. As you might have guessed, when the northern hemisphere is tilted towards the Sun, it receives more sunlight and warmth. This is when it is around June – our summer! Then, when we have completed around half an orbit – six months have passed and it is December – the northern hemisphere is tilted away from the Sun, meaning we receive less warmth and sunlight. This is our winter.

See the next page for a visual representation of this effect.

EARTH AND SPACE

Seasons in the northern hemisphere

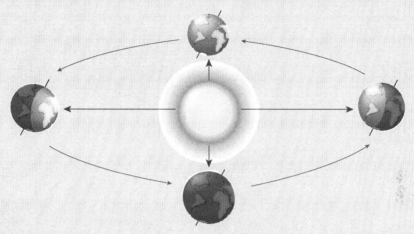

The Moon

The Moon is many times smaller than the Earth, and constantly moves in orbit around us, as the Earth does around the Sun. The time it takes for the Moon to complete its journey around the Earth is 28 days. Humans have used the lunar cycle as a guide to create our months.

As the Moon travels around the Earth, the half of it that faces the Sun is always lit up. However, it appears to change shape in the sky as we see it. This is because we see different amounts of the illuminated part as the Moon orbits Earth:

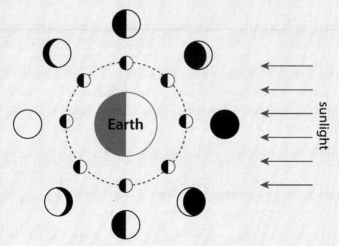

EARTH AND SPACE

3. Human understanding of space

Nowadays, it is common knowledge that the Sun is at the centre of our solar system. However, for centuries it was believed that Earth was at the centre, and everything else revolved around us. It wasn't until the 17th century that scientists and mathematicians were able to prove that this wasn't the case.

Of course, there are still huge amounts that we still do not know about space and the universe; it is impossible to say what humans of the future will come to understand!

See below for a timeline of how human understanding of space has developed:

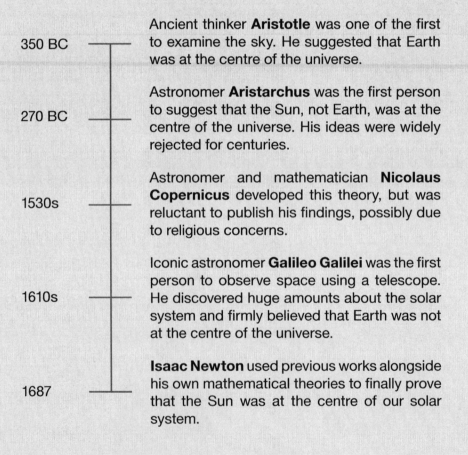

350 BC	Ancient thinker **Aristotle** was one of the first to examine the sky. He suggested that Earth was at the centre of the universe.
270 BC	Astronomer **Aristarchus** was the first person to suggest that the Sun, not Earth, was at the centre of the universe. His ideas were widely rejected for centuries.
1530s	Astronomer and mathematician **Nicolaus Copernicus** developed this theory, but was reluctant to publish his findings, possibly due to religious concerns.
1610s	Iconic astronomer **Galileo Galilei** was the first person to observe space using a telescope. He discovered huge amounts about the solar system and firmly believed that Earth was not at the centre of the universe.
1687	**Isaac Newton** used previous works alongside his own mathematical theories to finally prove that the Sun was at the centre of our solar system.

Question 1

Look at the following diagram representing our solar system. You will notice that there are some planets missing. Use your knowledge of the order of the planets to complete the diagram, by drawing the missing ones and labelling them. Don't worry about getting the sizes to scale!

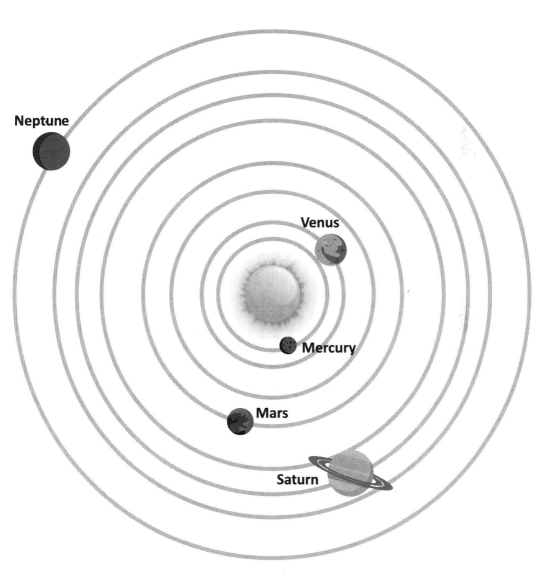

Question 2

Answer the following multiple choice questions by circling either **a)**, **b)** or **c)**.

1. The Earth takes this many days to complete its orbit around the Sun.

    a. 365

    b. 28

    c. 52

2. The Earth spins on its axis…

    a. For half of the year

    b. It never spins on its axis

    c. Constantly

3. From around June, the northern hemisphere is tilted _____ Earth.

    a. Away from

    b. Towards

    c. At a right angle from

4. While the northern hemisphere is experiencing summer, the southern hemisphere is in…

    a. Winter

    b. Summer as well

    c. Darkness

5. Compared to the Earth, the Moon is…

    a. Much smaller

    b. About the same size

    c. A little bit bigger

6. Throughout its 28 day orbit around the Earth, the Moon…

    a. Appears the same size in the sky

    b. Appears to change size in the sky

    c. Actually changes size

Question 3

Blaze and Freddie are arguing about human understanding of space. Consider what they both say and decide who you agree with!

Blaze says: "As science and technology slowly developed, human understanding of the universe developed with it."

Freddie says: "People thousands of years ago were stupid to believe that the Earth was at the centre of the solar system."

Who do you most agree with?

_____

_____

_____

_____

_____

_____

ANSWERS TO EARTH AND SPACE

Question 1

Your diagram should look something like this:

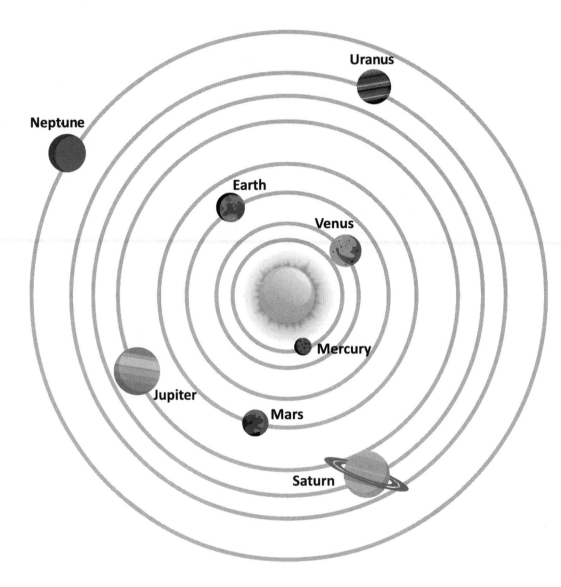

Question 2

1. a)
2. c)
3. b)
4. a)
5. a)
6. b)

Question 3

What Blaze says is undoubtable, but Freddie expresses an opinion. While it would be possible to argue that the belief that Earth was at the centre of the universe is a stupid one, we must appreciate that people thousands of years ago did not have the technology we possess today to examine the universe. Early thinkers like Aristotle actually paved the way for modern scientists by being the first to attempt to explain our solar system and universe.

HOW ARE YOU GETTING ON?

WANT MORE SCIENCE PRACTICE QUESTIONS?

How2Become has created other FANTASTIC guides to help you and your child prepare for their Key Stage Two (KS2) Science SATs.

These exciting guides are filled with fun and interesting facts for your child to engage with, to ensure that their revision is fun, and their learning is improved!

Invest in your child's future today!

FOR MORE INFORMATION ON OUR KEY STAGE 2 (KS2) GUIDES, PLEASE CHECK OUT THE FOLLOWING:

WWW.HOW2BECOME.COM

NEED MORE HELP WITH OTHER SCHOOL SUBJECTS?

Get Access To

FREE

Psychometric Tests

www.PsychometricTestsOnline.co.uk